For Kaye: The Afterlife

by

Robert Hamblin

ISBN: 9798688202175

"The rain to the wind said,
'You push and I'll pelt.'
They so smote the garden bed
That the flowers actually knelt,
And lay lodged--though not dead.
I know how the flowers felt."
– Robert Frost

"Everything you love will probably be lost,
but in the end, love will return in another way."
– Franz Kafka

"Wear me as a seal upon your heart,
as a seal upon your arm;
for love is as strong as death."
–*Song of Solomon* 8:6

Contents

Epilogue

Preface

For weeks, even months, after Kaye's death I simply wanted to die. I couldn't imagine life without her. I just wanted to be with her. That's a common feeling, I'm told, among those who survive a spouse one has lived with for many, many years—in my case with Kaye, just two months short of sixty.

I know Kaye would not want me to feel like this. She would want me to live on, to be here for the kids and grandkids, to find a purpose for my remaining days. I told myself this every day. But then I would see her picture on the mantel, or touch a book or some other object she once held, or walk past the flower beds she planted and tended, or hear one of her favorite songs, and the breath would go and the weeping resume. I was smothering in my grief.

My grief was compounded, I'm sure, by the manner of Kaye's death. She died of Alzheimer's, which robbed her of personhood and us of our last two years together. I was her principal caregiver, and I watched over her month after month as she descended into darkness— and as our two prayers were answered: hers, that she be allowed to remain at home, and mine, that I would live long enough to take care of her. In the end her death was merciful and an answer to both our prayers: I lived to take care of her, and she died peacefully in her sleep lying beside me.

I could accept her death because for her last few months she was helpless—confined to a hospital bed, unable to speak or otherwise communicate with others, unaware of her surroundings, dependent on me to feed, bathe, and medicate her. No one would choose, for oneself or for someone else, to continue to live under such conditions. Nevertheless, I was angry and bitter about the Alzheimer's, which day by relentless day was destroying Kaye's mind and body and leaving her a hollow shell of the wonderful, vibrant, caring person she had always been.

I had always considered myself a person of faith, but now that faith was being challenged and cast very much in doubt. Had the Alzheimer's fallen upon me, I think I might have accepted it more readily. I might even have reasoned that I deserved it. I am not a good person. I am selfish, vain, arrogant, guilty of many sins, confessed and unconfessed. But Kaye was a good person, a saint. How could such an undeserved fate befall such a good person? It wasn't fair. During our ordeal I often thought of the ancient story of Job, but my sentiments tended more toward the viewpoint of his wife than that of Job. "Curse God and die" was no longer a misspoken line in an old story.

Perhaps because I was so intimately involved in her care, and because the horrible memories of the devastating effects of the Alzheimer's were so fresh and raw, I had trouble focusing on all the good years and great experiences we had shared. I didn't know what to call it at the time, but counselors subsequently explained that I had a severe case of survivor's guilt. For days I had to force myself to eat, and I couldn't bear even to look at the foods in the refrigerator and cabinet that I had fed her during her final weeks—applesauce, yogurt, oatmeal, fruit cocktail, ice cream, popsicles. Any leftovers or unopened containers of such items I threw into the garbage.

Nighttime was the worst. I couldn't read, write, watch television, or sleep. The only antidote was to walk long distances or work for hours in the yard to exhaust myself, and even then I could not fall asleep until 2 or 3 a.m.

The covid-19 pandemic, of course, further complicated my situation. I despaired that we had not been able to give Kaye a decent funeral, being limited to a short graveside ceremony for just the immediate family; and now the inability to go shopping or attend church or visit friends deepened my depression. Caring for Kaye had been an around-the-clock task; with her gone I could find nothing purposeful to fill the empty space.

During Kaye's final weeks I lay beside her every night and voiced the same prayer: "God, give her peace. Give her comfort. Give her an untroubled mind. Give her strength." After her death, that became my prayer: "God, give me comfort. Give me peace. Give me an untroubled mind. Give me strength."

Gradually, though at the time it seemed an eternity, I began to recover. It is commonly said that "time heals all wounds." But that's not true. The deep wounds of grief never heal. They will always be there, scars that we may learn to hide from the world but which forever after will pierce our hearts. Maybe that's the way it should be. Remembrance of pain is no less a measure of love than remembrance of joy.

Relatives and friends came to my rescue. Our children, Laurie and Stephen, were constant anchors of strength and encouragement, both before and after Kaye's death. Kaye's brother and sister-in-law called frequently, as did my Mississippi kin and a nephew from Utah who had lost a son in an automobile accident and thus knew the indescribable depths of sorrow. Friends from church came by to bring food. Others called or sent cards and emails. I have never been a fan of social media, but in my seclusion I discovered that the internet was a useful way to stay tethered to the outside world.

Over time the good memories began to displace, or at least balance, the bad ones. For some reason I could not look at photos of Kaye and me. But I rediscovered the pleasure of reading, and I especially, and initially, enjoyed reading things she had written—the children's story she wrote and illustrated for our granddaughters, her account of growing up on a Mississippi farm, the book she wrote about the pioneer family associated with our historic home, the biography of her father that she and I co-authored. Concerning the last, I fondly recalled the several trips we made to Mississippi to research the book, especially the day we sat together in the musty basement of the Alcorn County courthouse leafing through the pages of old newspapers. She always laughed about that.

Other memories began to scroll through my consciousness like a video unfolding on a screen, and now the images were those of a happy, blessed life. Of our high school and college days together. Of our marriage and our first teaching jobs in Baltimore. Of our graduate studies at Ole Miss and our move to Cape Girardeau. Of the adoption of our two children, and later the arrival of our grandchildren and great-grandchildren. Of our life in Cape Girardeau and at Southeast Missouri State University and First Baptist Church. Of our travels across the United States and overseas, especially our two semesters in London, her favorite city. We had known a marvelous life together, far beyond what two country kids from Mississippi could ever have dreamed or imagined.

Writing also played a large role in my recovery. Although there were times when the depression made it impossible to sit at a computer and record my thoughts, over time I was able to return to writing and it became a type of therapy for me. That had been true of my previous book, *Darkness Descending*, which chronicled the onset and advancement of Kaye's Alzheimer's, and now the pattern was repeating itself.

I've often wondered why writing is so much help to me in times of stress. I think it's more than an escape mechanism. I think it possibly has to do with issues of control, or at least perceived control. Life so very often spins out of control; but writers are in control of the blank page or screen, and words flow at their command. I've been reminded of that again during Kaye's illness and death. Of course the moment or minutes or hours spent in

creativity are in one sense illusionary, since the real world
will shortly return with all its uncertainty and angst. But
when I write about Kaye, she's still with me. We write to
mend our broken hearts.

There is an old Christian concept known as *felix
culpa*, the "happy mistake" or "fortunate fall." It holds
that something good can come out of even the worst of
experiences: "God works in all things for good." It's the
overarching theme of Milton's *Paradise Lost* and
Shakespeare's *The Tempest* and many other literary and
theological works. I had used the theme myself in my
book of poems, *Dust and Light*, and I considered it one of
my fundamental convictions.

But Kaye's terrible illness and death had called that
belief into question. I could not see anything positive
resulting from such tragic circumstances. I thought,
maybe the existentialists are right in viewing life as a
theater of the absurd. Kaye had died on Good Friday and
was buried two days after Easter. That Easter setting
became the pattern of my existence. However, for a long
time I was trapped in the death and burial part of the
story: no resurrection seemed possible.

But resurrection did happen. And I am aware of
two precise moments when I realized it had. The first was
when I visited Kaye's grave after a monument had been
installed. Because of the covid-19, there had been an
unusually long delay in getting that accomplished. During
that delay the grave site was a sad and desolate place—
the raw dirt, decaying flowers, no marker of any kind since
even the temporary identification had been damaged by

the caretaker's mower and Kaye's name card blown away by the wind.

But the presence of the monument brought a degree of closure and peace to my mind. Maybe it was simply knowing that a block of solid granite would verify Kaye's existence for perhaps centuries to come. Or maybe it was seeing my name there beside hers, reminding me that I would soon lie beside her once again.

The second moment was preternatural, and will always remain a mystery to me. One Sunday morning I awakened with a tune and a stanza of lyrics to a song running through my head. As I dressed I kept singing the song to myself so I would not forget the tune. I went straight to the computer and within fifteen minutes had composed the following:

One of These Days

This world's gonna turn again
        Yea Glory!
This world's gonna turn again
        Yea Glory!
One of these days the gloom will pass
Better days will come at last
This world's gonna turn again
        Yea Glory!

This earth's gonna shine again
        Yea Glory!
This earth's gonna shine again
        Yea Glory!

One of these days the clouds will pass
Better days will come at last
This earth's gonna shine again
        Yea Glory!

This heart's gonna love again
        Yea Glory!
This heart's gonna love again
        Yea Glory!
One of these days the grief will pass
Better days will come at last
This heart's gonna love again
        Yea Glory!

This soul's gonna live again
        Yea Glory!
This soul's gonna live again
        Yea Glory!
One of these days the Lord will come
And welcome this old sinner home
This soul's gonna live again
        Yea Glory!

No one will ever dissuade me from the belief that the lessons from the monument and the song were messages that Kaye sent me. Resurrection is possible, and real. My long dark night of the soul was over. With Kaye's spirit beside me, I would live out what life remained to me with renewed resolve and purpose.

Death

Buttons

First it was names and words.
Then the computer
and the cell phone.

Now, as I watch you
try to dress yourself,
it's buttons and zippers
you struggle with.

I try to be patient
as I would with a child,
knowing you need to do this
by yourself.

Sometimes you can,
and I revel in your success,
telling myself
that you're getting better.

More often
I have to finish the task
for you.
You always smile
and say thank you,
and I turn quickly away
so you will not see
my tears.

Time

Live in the moment,
we are told,
as if that were the secret
to a fulfilling life.

But victims of Alzheimer's
live only in the moment,
shut off from their past,
unaware of the future,
locked in the prison
of the present.

Watching and conversing
with Kaye, I am reminded
that time is a continuum,
that every present moment
also contains the past and the future,
that our very identity
is defined by a perception
of time as indivisible, a oneness
that cannot be separated.

Amputate an arm or a leg
and you are still you.
Sever time and you are nobody.

Each Morning

Each morning I help Kaye
repossess her world,
and herself.

We sit on the side of the bed
while I explain
who she is, who I am,
what our relationship is,
where we are,
what we will do today.

On good days
the lesson takes;
on bad days, most days now,
I must repeat the narrative
over and over.

I ask myself
what it must be like
to lose yourself every night
and have to find yourself again
every morning.

And I wonder, fear quaking
in my heart, how much longer
it will be until you cannot find
yourself at all, being lost
forever.

This Facility

"The people at this facility
are very kind and helpful.
They're not professionals,
but they all do a good job."

I no longer try to correct
Kaye's misconceptions
about this house, our house,
or about me, the husband
she thinks is one of several
workers who care for her.

I live now for those moments
of recognition, fewer and fewer,
when she remembers who I am.

"Let me look at your face,"
she says, holding it
between her two hands,
smiling at me.
"You're Bobby," she says.

"Yes," I reply, "your Bobby."
But knowing that all too soon,
I'll be lost to her again.

Good Friday, 3 a.m.

I rise from beside her
to administer her medications.
I see that she is unusually still
and quiet, mouth half-open and unmoving,
no breath and, when I check, no pulse.
But her body is still warm, so I know
she has died just minutes before.
I take her hand in mine,
kiss her lips, and recite the 23rd Psalm.

The nurse had said it would be like this,
since she had stopped eating
and her body was shutting down.
"Just days, maybe hours,"
he had told us yesterday.

I call Laurie and Stephen,
who have been waiting with me,
and leave them with their mother
while I go into the library to be alone.
I feel a terrible remorse and guilt
that I was not standing beside her,
holding her hand, when she died.
But we had already, weeks ago,
had to say our goodbyes:
I can't even remember now
when she was last responsive
to my voice and touch.

But with the sadness I also feel relief
that her long battle with Alzheimer's
is finally over, and gratitude
that my constant prayers
for the past two years have been answered:
that she would die peacefully at home
and that I would live long enough
to take care of her.

Now her suffering is over.
And mine begins.

An Easter Like No Other

Here no stone
has been rolled away.
The grief of Calvary
still smothers the heart.

Because of covid-19,
Laurie, Stephen, and I
stand alone
in an empty chapel:
no flowers,
no family mementos
on display,
no friends and relatives
to provide comfort
and encouragement.
Just three grieving mourners
beside a casket
and a corpse.

This is Resurrection Sunday,
but I find no resurrection here.

Rearranging the Furniture

The hospital bed and the wheelchair
are gone, reclaimed by the providers
to use with other patients.
I remove dishes, utensils, blankets,
and caretaking supplies.
I discard unused medications.
Stephen helps me dismantle
the king-size bed and move it
back to the upstairs bedroom.
The parlor has been restored
to the design of your choosing.

More rearranging will be required,
and that will be harder.
Tonight I will sleep in our bedroom
for the first time in over a year.
Sometime during the night
I will awaken and turn to you,
and you will not be there.
Where have you gone, my darling,
and how can I live without you?

The Hawks

The black shadows
of the circling hawks
glide across the green lawn.

I watch the shadows.
I do not yet have the heart
to watch your hawks
dipping and climbing
in the blue sky.

They've cut down
the dead oak tree next door
where, every late afternoon,
the hawks liked to gather.

I think of how we loved
to sit together on the front porch
and count them,
sometimes as many as six,
perched at the top of the tree.

Where the tree stood
there is now only empty space,
nothing worth seeing.

Today I follow the dark shadows.
Tomorrow I will try again
to look up at the hawks.

Burial

Graveside Service

This is not the way to have a funeral.
No friends paying their respects,
no eulogy expressing love and tribute,
none of the hymns she sang for others.
Just our small family
standing beside the casket,
two of our dearest friends,
wearing masks and gloves,
seated in a car at the edge of the lot,
the minister, three funeral home assistants.

I've brought a cane to lean on,
more to steady my emotions
than my body.
I hear the minister's voice
but not the words.
I strain but cannot hold back the tears.

Kaye helped me pick this spot
before her Alzheimer's became worse.
Near two tall evergreens,
a gently sloping hillside with scattered trees,
not far from our home of many years
and the streets she daily walked
with me or with Nellie, the hound.
An attractive site, but today
the just-blooming dogwood and redbud
mock the barreness of my heart,
the inconsolable sorrow of my soul.

Laurie and Stephen help me to the car,
and with them I leave the cemetery,
toward the nothingness that lies ahead.

The Grave

It has been weeks,
but because of the delay
caused by the corona virus pandemic,
there is yet no monument
on Kaye's grave.

Even the temporary marker
has been broken
by the caretaker's mower
and the name plate
blown away by the wind.

I visit the spot,
smooth the raw dirt,
replace the decomposed flowers
with roses from her garden,
praying that she understands
and forgives the neglect.

Survivor's Guilt

I haven't eaten again today.
I have to force myself to eat,
and I can't bear to even look
at the foods I spoon fed you
during your last months.
All of the leftover containers
of those—applesauce, oatmeal,
yogurt, fruit cocktail, ice cream—
have been thrown into the garbage.

And it's not just food.
I can't look at your photographs,
and I weep as I dust your curios
and weed your flower beds.

I know you would not want
me to feel like this,
and some would consider it weakness
and a lack of faith.

But I can't help myself,
and is not my pain another measure
of my love for you?

The Stone Breakers, 2010

The front sidewalk was breaking up,
so we decided to replace it
with designer stones.

I wielded the sledge hammer
and Laurie carted off
the broken pieces of concrete.
You watched carefully to ensure
the safety of your flower beds.

It was Laurie's idea to replicate
Courbet's famous painting.
We held the pose
while you snapped the picture.

Laurie and I scattered sand
over the surface
and laid in the stones—
crooked!

Then you brought us string
and instructed us on how
to lay a plumb line.

You were our plumb line,
in everything.
Now there are no straight lines
without you.

In My Dreams Now

In my dreams now
someone is always lost.
Usually it's me,
sometimes it is you.

I'm driving on an unfamiliar road,
not recognizing any landmark,
not knowing to turn right or left.
Or I'm walking with you in the mall,
and when I turn to ask you a question
you are not there.

I now live in a foreign country
and I do not speak the language.
I live in a town
where nobody knows my name.

With Moo

I still take walks with Moo.
We follow the path you and I did,
along Broadway, through the park,
around the courthouse, and back home.

I sit, as we did, on the bench
in front of the courthouse
and watch the barges on the river.
I talk to Moo about you,
things you said and did:
window shopping in the antique stores,
laughing at Moo's antics with the squirrels,
identifying the birds by their songs.

Maybe one day soon
we'll take a different route,
but for now, and maybe for a long time,
I need you with us,
every step of the way.

Resurrection

Saying No to Death

Memory is a means
of saying No to death;
Faulkner learned it from Proust,
and I learned it from both of them.
So when there's no memory,
Is there then no life?
Yes, if there is someone else
who remembers.

I will remember for you.
As long as I am alive,
you are alive as well.
In all that I remember,
you will be present.
Our two hearts as one,
then and always.

Let's take a long walk
together.

Riding Westward, 1983

Once,
in another country,
I traveled
a golden highway.

The sun,
in curious afterthought
to cloud and shower,
tilted a chalice
beyond a distant hill
and slid its surplus splendor
down a narrow sluice
of pavement,
becoming, for an instant,
one with earth.

It seemed
I could follow
that happy road
right into eternity.

Then heaven withdrew.
We drove on, into darkness.

Where the road led,
or what I was doing there,
I do not recall.

I remember only
the woman I loved sat beside me,
and the gold, such gold.

San Francisco, August 1977

After the cable cars
tumbled us, laughing,
up and down hills
to Chinatown and back,

After the minstrel crowds
on Fisherman's Wharf
mingled their merriment
with our love,

After the Golden Gate
funneled us, transformed,
beyond the city,
across the bay,

We walked, at dusk,
a mile to the shore
and watched the sun
go golden with the sea.

The waves,
in jubilation of our joy,
turned cartwheels
on the sand.

Travelers

In motel restaurants
I see them,
solitary as poets,
sipping their loneliness
like wine, dancing
their wills on the bold
incontinence of lounge music,
floating desire to distant rooms
where deep-mouthed waitresses
open their legs, joyfully,
to the mother-womb
of all returnings.

Newspaper in hand,
homeless as an unclaimed tip,
they walk the dull corridor,
turn the key,
bury their tameless eyes
in single, silent beds.

And always, when I see them,
I think of you, and feel
the visible touch of your
too, too invisible hands.

Special Outing

Remember the surprise getaways
we planned for each other?
Often just dinner and a movie,
but sometimes an out-of-town trip.
We would alternate the surprises.
Once you took me to Paducah
for a concert at the Carson Center.
I took you to Memphis,
where we had spent our honeymoon.
As we drove the other
would try to guess the destination.
Fun times!

Today I am taking you
to Trail of Tears State Park,
to revisit one of your favorite places.
It's October, and the hillsides are ablaze
with every color of the spectrum.
We'll walk to the overlook
and watch a slow barge
hauling its freight north toward St. Louis.
We used to follow the railroad track
and cut through the woods
to the old stone quarry,
but access to the quarry
is no longer allowed.

So today we'll just sit here together
for a while, holding hands, a cool breeze

livening our bodies and spirits,
letting time, like the ancient river below us,
go slowly, and wishing this day
would never end.

A Single Flower

That was the year some said
spring would never come.
Close-fisted April held Easter
hostage under threat of snow.
The persecution of sun seemed endless.

Even the dogwood which is first
to blossom acquiesced to days of gloom.
Or so we thought—until we chanced
to glimpse a single flower, one
splendid inflorescence, impatient
with nature's delay, breaking winter's
strangling hold to possess the air.
Except for this one unaccountable utterance,
the whole tree spoke not a single word.

We called the children to witness
the anomaly. Together, fascinated
and strangely renewed, we watched
the eager pinkness warm the sun,
loose the frozen gears of the season,
peel the silence from the tight-throated days.

A Benediction

Do you remember
that night when, after making love,
we lay quietly and listened
to the approaching storm?

Thunder splashed lightning
across the sky, blowing fear
past the inner edges of our souls.
Deep, untaught terror
chased the children to our door,
and together we sought the candled
safety of our basement room.

There, the children wrapped
in our too human arms,
we watched a violent wind
twist and thrash a climbing rosebush
against the window.

This was no earthly menace,
forcing entry, but something far more
definite and sinister.
How anything could endure such rage
we hardly knew.

Then we, and nature, slept.
The next morning we stood
among wasted leaves and petals
and marveled at a white rose,
perfect in bloom, graced

beyond the threatening night,
nestling in the shelter of the eaves.

In That Winter

In that winter of my cold despair
we sat and watched the vagrant birds
feeding outside our kitchen window.
Daily they came in chattering herds—
woodpecker, cardinal, finch, and sparrow,
junco, thrasher, towhee, lark—all were there,
braiding their busy brightness on every limb
of the dogwood's flayed and joyless stem.

You laughed at the nervous titmouse all eye
for the hawking jay, scolded the selfish siskin race,
too jealous to share their discovered grace.

Once the stately grosbeak, stranger to our little band,
pasted its color across a blackbird's gloomy stare;
and once I found you, patient as the snow,
taming the electric chickadee with your hand.

All those days they came in ceaseless need,
and hourly you replenished their store of seed.
So too in that winter, as you know, did I—
like your friends the robin and the dove,
finding rest and hope of sunny April sky
in the windless cedars of your perfect love.

Love on the Escalator

Riding the escalator
rising from the Underground,
I reach behind me,
as I often do,
to hold your hand.

Getting no response,
I stroke your side
and hip lightly
with my fingers.

Then I hear your voice
from below: "Bob,
that's not me."

I turn to see
a startled, confused
young man
standing behind me,
and three steps below, you,
embarrassed, laughing.

Fortunately,
he laughs too.

Traveling
(After the Fashion of John Donne)

We need no map
or guidebook
for this journey.
Or rather, we'll be
each other's map
and guide.

Let our hands be feet
to stroll through all the hills
and valleys of our passion,
north, south, east, and west,
and every compass point
in between.

Let my eyes be sun,
warming you along footpaths
and rippling streams
to waterfalls hidden
within the deep woods.

Let your lips be wind,
cooling my body
on a grassy knoll
where we linger
to feast on cheese and wine.

Let our hearts be birds,
diving into the lake
and flying to the tops

of the highest trees.

Let our thoughts be clouds,
floating, rising,
pure white and speechless,
against the blue sky.

Let our souls be air,
melted, fused, invisible,
contented to be joined together,
forever.

Sigmund Freud Walks in Regent's Park

Barefoot children
curl their toes
in the rich grass.

Young mothers
push their babies
in strollers,
shameless
in their pride.

Men lie on blankets,
naked to the waist,
sleeping with the sun.

Women,
veiled all winter,
now expose arms,
legs, faces, hair
to the breeze.

Lovers stroll
hand in hand,
wrap their bodies
about each other
on benches,
paddle canoes
across the lake.

Tonight
(or even sooner)

in bed
(or elsewhere)
someone
(you know who)
will have to do penance
for such a wanton
spring.
And not with prayers.

4th of July

Without you it's only noise
that frightens Moo
and explodes my heart.

But I'm recalling the times
we sat with the kids
on the cobblestone bank
and watched the fireworks display
over the Mississippi.

And the time we took
Stephen and the grandkids
to celebrate the 4th in New York.
After visiting Ground Zero
we watched the fireworks
light up the sky above the East River
and the Statue of Liberty.

The next day,
while Stephen took the girls
to tour the wax museum,
you and I stood in a long line
to buy gyros from a street vendor,
then sat on a park bench to enjoy them.
Two Mississippi kids still in awe
of the world and of each other.

Another Julia

Years from now
another Julia
will read your book
about her ancestor,
the original Julia,
and she will see you
sitting in the reading room
of the county archives
and climbing the hill
to the Bollinger family cemetery
and driving to St. Louis
to view old church records
and admiring the stained glass windows
in the first Julia's house,
and you will live again
in the enduring story you told.

Winter Storm Watch

All day the sleet
has fallen,
almost invisible,
but when I step outside
I hear its busy rattle
on the ground
and feel the icy spikes
against my hands and face,
driving me back inside
to join you at the kitchen table,
where we sit with cupped hands
around mugs of hot chocolate
and watch the birds
and squirrels quarrel
over the feeders
scattered about the deck.

There are worse ways
to spend a winter day.
In fact, I rather hope
the prognosticators are right
and the sleet will turn to snow
and the snow will continue all night,
blocking the streets
and shutting out the world
so tomorrow, again,
we, just the two of us,
can sit at the kitchen table

with hands cupped around mugs
of hot chocolate,
watching the birds and squirrels.

Holy Communion

—to Sister Mary Dolorine, SS.CC.

You've been gone a week,
but your presence is still with us,
as palpable as your parting gifts:
the white basket of red impatiens
now hanging from the dogwood beside our deck
and the lavender rose,
already bursting with its first buds
among Kaye's other flowers.

You wanted to assist in the planting,
so I prepared the soil,
shoveling out the dead remains of the one rose
that had not survived the hard winter,
and you and Kaye carefully placed
the new rosebush into the ground,
firmly packing the dirt
around its roots with your hands.
Then you, laughing but serious,
pronounced a blessing on our work,
and we went inside for a generous helping
of Kaye's biscuit pudding.

It was all so very ecumenical,
two Baptists and a Catholic nun
pointing nature toward a resurrection
and celebrating our triumph
with the sweetest communion
the tongue could ever know.

Tomorrow, here in Missouri,
we'll be thinking, with you in Hawaii,
of your beloved Father Damien
being honored by the Pope in Brussels.
We'll remember with what joy
you told us of the discovery of the healing miracle
that made his beatification possible.
And your explanation of how the event
had to be meticulously investigated and confirmed
by a panel of medical experts.
You'll recall how amused I was by that.
"You say he left his family and friends
in his native Belgium
and went to live among the lepers
on the Hawaiian island of Molokai,
where he stayed for sixteen years,
until he contracted the disease and died?
And your church has been searching for a miracle?"

Being Protestant,
and certainly no saint, as you well know,
I am not nearly so scrupulous
where miracles are concerned.
In fact, I find them everywhere.
As on that Sunday a few years ago
when we traveled with you by train
from Rome to Velletri to spend the day
with your dear friends the Sambrottas.
What a feast we shared:
of food and wine, music and laughter,

storytelling and friendship!

I wish we had thought
to plant a rose that day as well.

The House Eyes of Sibiu

The houses' eyes,
windows cut into the sloping roofs,
the eyes of God,
are always watching,
have been watching for centuries.

They've seen soldiers
on parade and at war,
street vendors shouting their wares,
children in bright uniforms
on their way to school,
lovers walking hand in hand,
nobility and peasants.

Today they watch the tourists
crowding the ancient square,
strolling from museum to museum,
listening to guides
speaking the history of Transylvania
in various languages.

If I were up there at this moment
looking down through those eyes,
I would spy an elderly couple
and a middleaged woman
following a man
across the cobblestone streets.
And I would know them
as myself, my wife, and our daughter

in the happy company
of our dear friend and host Didi.

And I would know that today
the eyes of God are smiling.

Beside the Maas

In Maastricht,
the oldest city in the Netherlands,
strolling beside the Maas,
we think of our rivers back home,
the Missouri, the Ohio,
and Old Man Mississippi,
reflecting how all rivers
flow to the sea,
and the sea to the sun,
then back to earth again.

Thus all rivers are one,
the Maas and the Mississippi,
though continents apart, the same.

It's good to walk with you
beside the Maas
and know that here or there,
now or then or time to come,
together or apart,
we are one.

Gingko Tree in Our Back Yard

Looking at the shimmering gold
pooling around the base of the trunk,
or walking on the soft, magical
carpet dropped from heaven,

I wonder at the regret
and resentment I felt a week ago
as the heavy wind and rain
stripped the branches bare.

Now I am reminded
how each season gives something
to the next, air gives back
to earth, loss equates with gain.

And so I rake the other leaves,
hauling them to curbside for pickup,
but I leave this golden circle,
for a few more days, undisturbed,

And I think how nature
is always true and fair:
spring, summer, autumn, winter,
perfection displaced by more perfection.

Like the passing seasons
of our enduring love,
metamorphosing in face and hands,
unchanging in mind and heart.

How could we know,
that young and innocent couple
of the wedding picture so many years ago,
the joy and happiness that are ours today.

Flower Garden

Taking a welcome break
from weeding and mulching
Kaye's flower garden,
I sit on a bench to rest
my aching knees
and admire my work.

Impatiens lie all about me
like colored tokens scattered
by children on the ground;
the profligate zinnias and marigolds
paint their bright orange and yellow
and red petals on a canvas
of green ferns, hostas, and lamb's ears.
A climbing trumpet vine
winds its blossoms around the arbor.
The hooped skirt of the morning glory
drapes the pole of the bird house.

To invite a fuller vista
of this awesome summer day,
I lean my head back
and look at the sky.
Soft white clouds,
unhurried by any duty or demand,
gently move to the east
against a field of deepest blue.

Martins dive high and low

for insects before retiring
for the night.
I close my eyes to rest,
but even in the embracing darkness
vision remains,
as though pasted to my eyelids:
flowers innumerable, and clouds,
and the purest blue sky.

Could it be that death
might be something like this?
I ask myself: merely a closing of the eyes
to allow a fuller, sharper memory to shape itself:
the blue snowcones of the hydrangea,
the cascading fountains of the liriope,
the deep purples of the pansies,
silver drops of water from the sprinkler
glistening on the leaves of every plant,
and a woman whom you love
standing in a wash of color
admiring a budding rose.

That should be heaven enough
for any man.

Wedding Ring

I still wear my wedding ring,
and will until I die.

It's not the original one.
That one, as you know,
had to be cut off
my jammed and swollen finger
after a sports injury,
and the jeweler failed
to restore it to its proper size.

Later I lost it
while working in the back yard,
and today it lies buried there
with a succession of pets,
a repaired water line,
and lots of good memories.

So you bought me another ring
and married me a second time,
still inexplicable to me
since I hadn't yet figured out
why you married me the first time.

I didn't tell you often enough
that I'm glad you did.

The Song

This morning I awakened to the song
you had given me in my sleep.
You told me to live again.
You told me that grief would pass
and better days would come.
You told me the world would shine again.
The song revives and emboldens my spirit.
It tells me you will continue
to be alive in me and I in you.
Till death do us part.

Epilogue

Dear Kaye

This has been a long trip.
I don't like traveling without you.
I'll be home soon.
Please wait up for me.
I can't wait to see you.
Love,
Bobby

www.ingramcontent.com/pod-product-compliance
Lightning Source LLC
Chambersburg PA
CBHW061301140726
47998CB00006B/2317